W9-BSQ-906

S is for Save the Planet

A How-to-Be Green Alphabet

Written by Brad Herzog and Illustrated by Linda Holt Ayriss

For editor Aimee Jackson, researcher Sharon Tregaskis, and publicist Audrey Mitnick.
Not only did they help make this book possible, they also have dedicated themselves to
green living in countless different ways. We can all learn from their example.

B. H.

To all the children of Bainbridge Island who helped me with this project.

L. H. A.

Sleeping Bear Press®
310 North Main Street, Suite 300
Chelsea, MI 48118
www.sleepingbearpress.com

© 2009 Sleeping Bear Press is an imprint of Gale, a part of Cengage Learning.

Printed and bound in Canada.

10 9 8 7 6 5 4 3 2

Library of Congress Cataloging-in-Publication Data

Herzog, Brad.
S is for save the planet : a how-to-be green alphabet / written by
Brad Herzog ; illustrated by Linda Holt Ayriss.
p. cm.
ISBN 978-1-58536-428-2
1. Environmental protection—Citizen participation—Juvenile
literature. 2. Green movement—Juvenile literature. I. Ayriss, Linda,
ill. II. Title.
TD171.7.H47 2009
333.72–dc22   2008037602

Mixed Sources
Cert no. SW-COC-001271
© 1996 FSC
FSC

Earth is a big blue marble
        floating in a void of space—
billions of years older
        than even the human race.

But the more than six billion people
        who call this planet our home
must take good care of it.
        That's the message of these poems.

This is an active alphabet.
        Yes, you can help save the earth!
Just think about our blue marble
        and what it's really worth.

A a

It might be said that the beginning of the modern environmental movement occurred when millions of Americans made their voices heard on a single day in 1970. They did so in support of a proposal by United States Senator Gaylord Nelson of Wisconsin. Senator Nelson proposed that April 22nd should be designated Earth Day—a day when people would recognize that the earth doesn't belong to us. Instead, we belong to the earth. On that day more than 20 million Americans participated in rallies and protests, making it the largest demonstration in the nation's history. Nearly ten thousand schools, two thousand colleges and universities, and hundreds of communities participated.

Although it wasn't the first environmental protest, Earth Day succeeded in raising a new level of awareness about our natural resources and the threat of pollution. Even the U.S. government got the message. Over the next ten years, Republicans and Democrats joined to create the Environmental Protection Agency and pass more than two dozen major laws to protect our air, water, public lands, food safety, and endangered species. But there remains much work to be done.

Appreciation for our planet—
that's our letter **A**.
Every April 22nd
we celebrate Earth Day.

Life everywhere is connected—
from land to sea to air.
We're all in this together,
so let's each do our share.

B is for a bright idea—
a bulb that lasts much longer.
It saves a lot more energy,
which makes our planet stronger.

B sure to turn off every light.
Computers and TVs, too.
We'll burn less harmful coal that way.
It's the least that we can do.

About half of all electricity in the U.S. is produced by coal-burning power plants, which release invisible gases into the air. These gases can get into rain clouds and fall back to Earth—a harmful phenomenon known as acid rain. The less energy we use, the less coal those power plants will have to burn.

One of the easiest ways to save energy is to change the lightbulbs in your house—from the traditional incandescent lightbulb (which has been used for more than a century) to a compact fluorescent light (CFL) or a light-emitting diode (LED), which is more efficient still. Both are more expensive than incandescent bulbs, but they last many times longer and are much more efficient, so they actually save money in the long run. Because CFLs include small amounts of potentially harmful mercury, it is important to be very careful while handling broken bulbs (see the Web Resources page at the back of this book).

There are many other ways to save energy around the house. Read next to a window instead of using a light. Dust light fixtures regularly. And turn off your video games and computers when you're not using them. Better yet, unplug them. Often, they're still draining electricity even when they're not turned on.

Every year, Americans drive more than one trillion miles in their cars. One trillion! It takes many thousands of years to even count that high! Car exhaust contributes greatly to air pollution. The average commuter consumes more than 300 gallons of gas each year. This produces more than three tons of harmful carbon dioxide, which causes problems like smog, acid rain, and global warming. But if two cars are replaced by a two-person carpool, that number is cut in half. Three people cuts it by two-thirds.

If you are traveling in a car, try to keep the windows closed to make it run more efficiently. And try to use the heat and air conditioning as little as possible. Of course, the best solution is not to drive at all. If one million people replaced a five-mile car trip with a bike ride once a week, carbon dioxide emissions would be reduced by nearly 100,000 tons per year. That would be far healthier for people and for the planet.

Conserve fuel. How? Let's C...
Create a cool carpool.
Share a ride to anywhere—
be it work, play, or school.

Don't make your parents drive you.
Instead, just ride a bike.
Glide along on a skateboard,
or simply take a hike.

The question is asked thousands of times each day at grocery stores everywhere: "Paper or plastic?" The best answer: Neither. Plastic bags are no good because they last so long. They don't rot, decay, or dissolve when they are thrown away. The typical American family of four uses about 1,500 plastic bags each year! In all, an estimated 500 billion to one trillion bags are used annually. As many as three percent of them wash out to sea, where sea animals often eat them and die.

Although paper bags can be recycled, they are harmful in other ways. They require the destruction of millions of trees each year, and paper bag manufacturing generates more air and water pollution and more solid waste than even the creation of plastic bags. So the next time you accompany an adult to the grocery store, bring along your own bags. People use bags made out of canvas, hemp, cotton, even nylon. And they can be reused time after time.

D d

D is a daily decision—
"Paper or plastic?" they ask.
Tell your parents, "Neither!"
Then give them a new task.

Do the planet a favor.
It's not much of a chore.
Bring your own bags with you
to the grocery store.

Many animals and plants are endangered.
Extinction—that's our letter E.
But what does this enormous problem
have to do with you and me?

Ask your parents not to buy things
made from coral or reptile skin.
And if we stay away from ivory,
the world's great elephants win.

Scientists estimate that by the year 2050, as many as one-third of all plants and animals may be driven to extinction, largely due to human influences. Many of these endangered plant species provide important medicines. For instance, a substance in the bark of a tree called the Pacific yew, native to the Pacific Northwest, has shown promise as a treatment for cancer. Still, many species remain endangered, including more than one thousand animals worldwide—everything from the black rhinoceros, the snow leopard, and the giant panda to the white-winged duck, the blue whale, and the silver shark.

Humans threaten these species by destroying their natural environments and introducing other incompatible plants and animals to their habitats. Often, animals are killed for profit. Thousands of endangered African and Asian elephants have been lost because they have been illegally hunted for their ivory tusks. And sometimes animals become endangered because of human carelessness. Dolphins are often accidentally caught in nets put out by tuna fishermen. So make sure your family eats dolphin-safe tuna and stays away from items like ivory jewelry or tortoiseshell glasses or coral souvenirs that come from endangered species.

More than 85 percent of the world's energy production comes from burning fossil fuels like coal, oil, and natural gas. These are the relics of ancient plants and animals that fell into swamps and oceans and were buried under layers of sand and clay. Over hundreds of millions of years, the layers piled up and turned to rock. The resulting pressure, combined with the heat in the earth's crust, turned that ancient life into fossil fuels. When the fuels are burned, the carbon that had been locked in their tissue is released as carbon dioxide, a gas that pollutes air, water, and forests and causes global warming.

In recent decades people have begun to examine other alternatives for creating energy, such as solar power, wind power, and hydropower. Many dedicated environmentalists install solar panels on their houses or put up windmills nearby. Perhaps someday you might do that. Or maybe you'll invent a better way to turn sun, wind, or water into energy.

When plants and animals died long ago,
they were buried under sand and clay.
These fossils were heated by the earth.
They're our F—fossil fuels—today.

Coal, oil, and natural gas
seemed like an energy solution.
But burning them causes problems—
way too much pollution.

Global warming—that's our **G**.
Earth is getting hot in a hurry.
After millions of cool years,
the planet's fever is our great worry.

"Greenhouse gases" fill the air
when fossil fuels are burned.
They're warming things up way too much.
Let's cool it. Let's show we've learned.

Gg

According to the World Meteorological Organization, the top 11 warmest years since 1850 have occurred since 1995. In fact, temperatures are higher everywhere—from the depths of the ocean to the upper atmosphere. Most scientists agree that, for the first time in history, human behavior is changing Earth's climate.

The earth is surrounded by a blanket of invisible gases—like carbon dioxide, nitrous oxide, and methane—that trap heat from the sun and keep us warm. But by burning things like forests and fossil fuels, we are creating far more of these gases than the earth's system can absorb. These "greenhouse gases" prevent heat from being released to outer space, causing a warming effect much like a greenhouse where plants are grown. This could have dire consequences in the future, including more severe storms, frequent droughts, and the melting of polar icecaps, which is already causing ocean water levels to rise. Island countries and coastal cities would be threatened. They would be in danger of being submerged by the sea if water levels rise only a few feet!

With less than five percent of the world's population, the United States produces nearly one-fourth of the earth's greenhouse gases.

H is for helium balloons.
    Hold on! Don't let it fly!
It just might hurt an animal
    when it falls from the sky.

    Our litter can be harmful
      to all of Earth's creatures.
    Tell your parents what can happen.
      While you're at it, tell your teachers!

Perhaps you have accidentally let a balloon go, watching it drift with the wind. It may have been fun at the time, but it's no fun for animals. A helium balloon can be blown hundreds of miles. Often, it ends up in the ocean, where the salt water washes off the balloon's color and sea animals mistake it for a jellyfish. They eat it and soon starve to death because the balloon blocks their stomachs. So if your school plans to celebrate a special occasion with a balloon launch, tell them about the dangers. Who says kids can't teach teachers a thing or two?

Many kinds of littering can harm animals. For example, squirrels may stick their heads into small plastic containers and get stuck there. Discarded chewing gum can be dangerous for wild animals because it can get caught in feathers and fur and possibly even cause suffocation if swallowed. And birds, fish, and turtles can strangle or starve after getting stuck in six-pack rings, those plastic circles that hold together canned beverages. So snip those six-packs, and throw trash in the trash can where it belongs. Better yet, buy cans without plastic rings. If the animals could talk, they would thank you.

H
h

I i

I? That's insulation in your house.
Keep the heat down. Wear a sweater.
It's an easy way to conserve energy.
Isn't that always better?

Be a private I—
a leak investigator.
You can save your parents money.
They'll surely thank you later.

Nearly half of your parents' energy bill each month goes toward heating and cooling your home. In the United States this is responsible for producing more than 150 million tons of carbon dioxide annually. But there are energy-saving ways to keep your home cool in the summer and warm in the winter without having to turn up the air conditioning or the heat. In summer's heat, you can keep the shades pulled down and use a fan. During winter's chill, you can dress warmly, install storm windows, and make sure the house is well insulated. In fact, you can be a detective. With an adult's help, use a candle to test for drafts under doors and around windows. By lowering the thermostat in the house just two degrees, your parents can save money each month and help prevent as much as 500 pounds of carbon dioxide from entering the atmosphere in just one year. Don't forget about the water heater, too. Many manufacturers set them at 140 degrees Fahrenheit, but 120 degrees is usually hot enough.

Over the past several decades, we have become a society that prefers disposable items (like paper napkins, plastic wrap, and aluminum foil) and lots of packaging. Have you ever noticed how much unwrapping of paper and plastic you have to suffer through after buying a new toy? When you and your family are shopping, you can help the environment by paying careful attention to what you purchase, and what you don't.

Nearly one-third of the garbage in landfills is packaging. That's garbage that wasn't even used! Look for sensibly packaged items. Sometimes you can even buy things without any packaging. Buy in bulk quantity, rather than single servings. Try to avoid disposable items, and practice *precycling*. That means buying something packaged in recyclable or already recycled materials. For instance, some cereal boxes are made of recycled cardboard. Recycled napkins and paper towels are available, too, although it is better to choose reuseable cloth ones instead. In fact, it's always good to look for items that can offer extended usage, such as rechargeable batteries. Remember, when you throw something away, it doesn't simply disappear.

J j

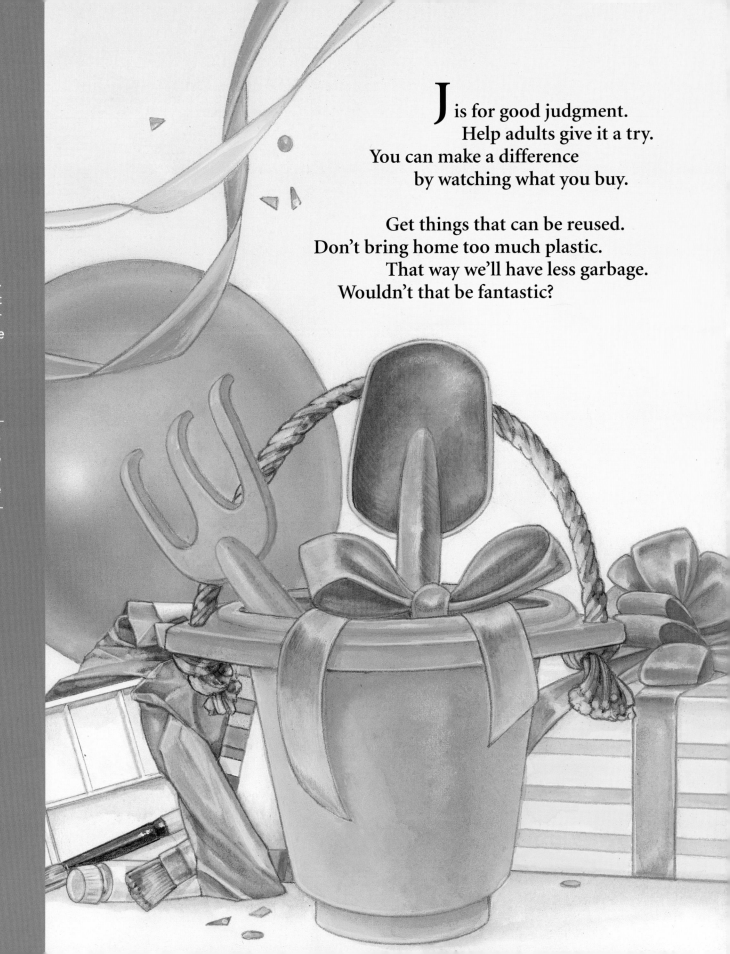

J is for good judgment.
Help adults give it a try.
You can make a difference
by watching what you buy.

Get things that can be reused.
Don't bring home too much plastic.
That way we'll have less garbage.
Wouldn't that be fantastic?

K is for kids, of course,
       who decide it's time to fix
local pollution problems.
       That's how they get their kicks.

You're never too young to do your part.
       All over the world, kids try
              to help protect the planet.
       They love it here. That's why!

Many earth-friendly organizations offer information just for kids on their Web sites, such as the Natural Resource Defense Council's Green Squad (www.nrdc.org/greensquad) and the Environmental Protection Agency's Kids Club (www.epa.gov/kids). There are also magazines—like *National Geographic Kids* and *Ranger Rick*—that celebrate nature. So you can participate. Read! Join! Act! Be a planet-saving hero!

All over the country, there are stories of kids who have made a difference. A seven-year-old in New York started a group called Kids Save the Ozone Project and won the President's Environmental Youth Award. A nine-year-old in Washington spurred creation of a recycling program at his school. A fourth-grade class in Illinois collected 471 pairs of old shoes that were used to make a bouncy, safe playground surface. A fifth-grade class in Michigan set up an event called Environmental Awareness Day that included games, skits, and information booths about pollution, conservation, and recycling. "We kids educated the grownups," said one student. So can you.

Food may travel thousands of miles
by truck, airplane, or train
before it even gets to you.
Now that's a silly food chain!

So why not buy from nearby farmers?
Eat locally. That's letter **L**.
Reduce pollution and packaging.
Fruits and veggies are fresher, as well.

Many environmentalists use the phrase "Think globally, act locally." That means you should be active in your community because you know it is planet-friendly. But it is also important to think globally and *eat* locally. A typical meal in the United States travels about 22,000 miles to reach your plate. The fish, meat, fruits, vegetables, and spices are often trucked or flown back and forth around the world as they are produced, packaged, and finally sold. That amounts to lots of "food miles," and the travel (along with the manufacture and disposal of the packaging) burns fuel and causes pollution.

That's why some people call themselves "locavores"—people who won't eat anything that has been grown or prepared more than 100 miles away. When you buy food at nearby farmers' markets, you are contributing both to cleaner air and to your community's well-being. Local markets also tend to have fresher fruits and vegetables, which may be contaminated with fewer pesticides than those in a supermarket.

Fresh Eggs

Kale

Ll

Just one percent of the planet's water supply is fresh water usable by humans. Some of it is located in rivers and lakes, but most of it is groundwater, which is generally pure water that fills the cracks and spaces underground. Over half of the U.S. population relies on groundwater for their source of drinking water, but it can be polluted by toxic liquids that seep into it—from underground storage tanks, garbage dumps, and pesticides and chemicals used in fertilized fields and industrial areas.

But individuals must be careful, too. Make sure nothing harmful is spilled on the ground, poured into a sink, or thrown away. One quart of motor oil, for instance, can seep into groundwater and pollute as much as 250,000 gallons of drinking water. Instead, store the container safely until you locate the nearest facility that recycles oil. Batteries, too, can be dangerous because some of them contain mercury, a toxic chemical that can leak into the ground when the batteries break apart. Recycle your batteries, and look for rechargeable ones that can be used many times.

M
m

Mercury and motor oil
are **M** in our alphabet.
In batteries and car engines,
    they're as harmful as it gets.

So dispose of these M's carefully.
        Don't just dump them. Please think.
They'll seep into our water supply.
        Then we'll have nothing to drink.

N is for a newspaper—
more paper than you need.
Save the world's great forests.
Recycle after you read.

Think of ways to stop a tree
from becoming logs and lumber.
Nearly a billion lost each year—
that's quite a nasty number.

Every year the average U.S. citizen uses more than 700 pounds of paper, and nearly 900 million trees are cut down to make that possible for all Americans. All kinds of paper products can be recycled—from newspapers and notebook paper to cardboard boxes and paper bags. Recycling paper doesn't only reduce pollution by saving trees. The *re-creation* of paper requires less energy and water and causes less acid rain and water pollution than the *creation* of paper. When paper is recycled, it is shredded and mashed into something called pulp, which is then turned back into paper. But in general, paper can only be recycled three to five times before its fibers break down. So it is important to think about other ways of reusing it as much as possible. Make use of both sides of a piece of paper. Use newspaper as protective packaging (instead of packing peanuts). Ask catalog companies to take you off their mailing lists. You can also turn junk mail into scrap paper, or wrap gifts with the Sunday comics. After all, you can be creative on paper, but you can also be creative *with* it.

O the lovely oceans,
     so beautiful and vast.
    But O no! Earth's mighty waters
     are being polluted fast.

    Plastic can harm animals
      throughout an ocean's reach.
     Save the world's sea creatures.
       Make time to clean a beach.

O o

Water covers approximately 70 percent of the earth's surface, but we haven't done a good job of keeping it clean. Our rivers, lakes, and oceans have been polluted by harmful chemicals and garbage, especially plastic, which is considered the number one hazard because of its threat to marine animals that mistake it for food. But there is something you can do about it. The next time you head to the beach, take a trash bag with you.

Each September since 1986, the Ocean Conservancy has organized its International Coastal Cleanup. Several hundred thousand volunteers of all ages descend on beaches, lakes, and streams all over the world to remove trash and debris, both on the shore-line and underwater. In just over two decades, the volunteers—and that includes kids!—have picked up more than 100 million pounds of debris along 170,000 miles of beaches and inland waterways. They also collect data about the types of debris that they find, which is analyzed and used to educate the public, businesses, and government officials about how to reduce the problem.

Trees are vital to the planet. We require oxygen and produce carbon dioxide by breathing. Trees absorb carbon dioxide and supply the air with oxygen. We also need as many trees as possible to balance the pollution created by factories and cars. A single tree can absorb one ton of carbon dioxide in its lifetime, so why not plant some yourself?

We must also save the world's rainforests. These warm, wet woodlands are home to more than half of the world's plants and animals and a source of many life-saving medicines. But throughout the past century, rainforests have been cut down at a frightening rate of 50 to 100 acres each day by people looking for lumber, grazing land, and farmland. We may be losing as many as 50,000 plant and animal species every year as a result. You can write to your representatives in Congress, asking for more rainforest protection. And you can ask your parents to do their part, too—for instance, by not buying wood products made out of tropical trees like mahogany, rosewood, and teak.

Pp

Pick a spot and leave your mark.
We've come to letter P.
Help our planet to breathe better.
P is plant a tree.

And P is protecting rainforests,
filled with animals, bugs, and plants.
Save these precious places.
Give nature a chance!

Q is a quest for a quiet place.
It's not too hard to find.
Get out in nature. Listen to birds.
Leave noise pollution behind.

Watch a sunset. Climb a peak.
Hike through massive trees.
Few sights anywhere on Earth
are as beautiful as these.

John Muir, one of America's earliest environmental heroes, loved to hike in the wilderness. "One day's exposure to mountains is better than cartloads of books about them," he said. Indeed, there is no substitute for seeing nature's wonders for yourself, whether it is the otherworldly trees of Sequoia National Park in California, the swamps of Everglades National Park in Florida, the grand rock formations of Arches National Park in Utah, or the dozens of other examples of protected wilderness throughout the United States and Canada. Just make sure that spectacular photos are all you take home with you.

If you can't get to a national park, there are hundreds of state and local parks—some not far from your own backyard. Go bird-watching, river-paddling, hill-climbing, or garden-strolling. Marvel at the serenity of a quiet forest. Watch how the setting sun brings out the vivid colors of a mountain range. Or simply sit on a sandy beach and watch the waves. Even in the city, there are birds, bugs, and trees to see. If you want to save the planet, it helps to appreciate it.

R r

Paper, plastic, glass,
aluminum cans, too.
Separate and save them.
You know just what to do.

R is our next letter.
Recycle relentlessly.
But reusing and reducing—
well, those are even better.

The three R's of responsible waste management are reduce, reuse, and recycle—and it is important to think of them in that order. Recycling is far better than simply throwing things away, whether this means paper, plastic, glass, aluminum, carpet, car batteries, or cell phones. After all, it takes 95 percent less energy to recycle aluminum than to create a new aluminum can. And the energy saved from recycling a single can is enough to run your TV for several hours. But reusing materials—whether this means converting glass jars into pencil holders, turning egg cartons into art projects, or keeping old toothbrushes to scrub hard-to-reach spots—is even better than recycling because it doesn't require any energy production. Best of all, however, is reduction. By reducing what you and your family buy, you are minimizing what is manufactured. That helps conserve natural resources. Overall, the goal is to get the most benefit from products while generating the least waste. That is why some people add another R to the list—rethink. The world is always open to new ideas.

What most of us think of as Styrofoam (a blue-tinted product invented by the Dow Chemical Company in the 1940s) is actually expanded polystyrene foam, which is white in color. Known for its insulating properties, it is used to make everything from coffee cups and coolers to pipe insulation and packaging materials. But it isn't easily recyclable, and it isn't biodegradable. That means it takes a *very* long time to decompose when it is thrown away—as long as hundreds of years. Its manufacture is harmful to the environment, and foam litter is destructive to sea life because it floats and is often mistaken for food.

Americans throw away 25 billion foam cups each year, so this is a big problem. Make sure your family avoids polystyrene foam products, whether in the form of egg cartons, packing peanuts, or takeout containers from restaurants. Some cities, such as San Francisco and Portland, have banned its use in restaurants, and in Canada there is a movement to eliminate it from the entire food and beverage industry.

S is for simply saying no
          to styrene foam containers.
Of all the save-the-earth suggestions,
          this one's a no-brainer.

          It cannot be recycled.
               It never disappears.
That foam cup that you're sipping from
          might last six hundred years!

T is trash—mountains of it!
Tons of it each day!
Cut down on that garbage.
Reduce what you throw away.

Don't simply toss out
old clothes or games or toys.
They could be something special
to other girls and boys.

Americans generate nearly 250 million tons of trash a year. That's about one ton for *each person* over the age of ten, and U.S. landfills (garbage dumps) are running out of room. Even if you're under ten, you contribute your share of trash, too. And you can also do something about reducing it. If you own stuff that can't be recycled and appears to be destined for the landfill, why not consider donating it instead of dumping it? If you don't want it anymore, share it with someone who does. And when you shop, consider buying used. Give these items a second life.

Donate used clothes and shoes to organizations that distribute them to those in need. Sell old books to a used-book store, or offer them to libraries that might be able to sell them and raise money for new books. Contribute used games and toys to hospitals, daycare centers, or other places where kids can take advantage of them. Give old blankets and towels to animal shelters. Or maybe you can organize your own garage sale. After all, one person's trash may be someone else's treasure.

Tt

U is unhealthy ultraviolet rays
sent toward Earth from the sun.
Way up high, the ozone layer
protects most everyone.

But lately, manufactured chemicals
have floated far up there.
They're eating up the ozone.
We must all take care.

U u

Ozone is a rare form of oxygen in which three oxygen atoms are linked together. It is good up high, but bad nearby. At ground level, ozone is caused largely by cars, trucks, and buses. It can be damaging to humans, animals, and plants because it is the principal component of smog, a brownish yellow haze that usually forms over cities during the summer. But high in the atmosphere, the ozone layer is important because it filters out certain ultraviolet rays from the sun. It is Earth's natural sunscreen, protecting us from harmful radiation by letting the good rays through and keeping the bad ones out.

However, much of the good ozone has gradually been destroyed by chemicals long used in everyday items like refrigerators and air conditioners. These gases have floated up into the atmosphere, causing a widening hole in the ozone layer. In 1987 the United States and more than 180 other countries adopted a treaty to gradually halt production and use of ozone-eating substances. Hopefully the hole in the ozone layer will shrink as our environmental awareness keeps growing.

Nearly 100 billion pounds of America's food goes to waste each year. So why not turn it into something useful? Instead of discarding food scraps, you can recycle them. And what helps in this earth-friendly activity? Earthworms, of course! They are some of nature's best recyclers.

Composting is a process in which organic material (made out of things that were once alive) such as kitchen scraps and yard waste are turned into compost, which is a nutritious soil-like material for plants. Vermicomposting simply adds red worms, which speed up the composting process by eating the rotting garbage and moving it through their digestive tracts. Simply line a bin with leaves or shredded paper, add worms, and gradually feed them everything from fruits and vegetables to coffee grounds and tea bags to plate scrapings and leftovers. Don't add meat, fish, or bones. One pound of worms (which is a lot) will eat about four pounds of food scraps in a week. In a few months you will have made your own natural fertilizer.

V
v

V is vermicomposting,
an environmental term
for turning garbage into soil
with the help of worms.

Don't throw away your food scraps.
Composting is much wiser.
Just watch the earthworms do their thing.
Trash becomes fertilizer.

The bad news: There are water shortages in many parts of the country and the world. The good news: There are many things you can do to conserve water. Make sure all faucets are completely turned off when not in use, and tell an adult if you find leaky ones. While brushing your teeth, only turn the faucet on when it's time to rinse. You can save five gallons of water that way. When doing dishes by hand, you can save up to 25 gallons by simply filling the kitchen sink instead of leaving the water running. You might also ask your parents if they would be willing to install low-flow showerheads, which cut the amount of water used in half.

Outdoors, too, you can make a difference. Avoid watering the lawn during the hottest, windiest times of day because the water will evaporate or be blown away. And make sure your sprinkler is watering the lawn, not the sidewalk! You can even use a rain barrel to collect rainwater from gutters. If you wash the family car, use buckets instead of a hose. You'll save as much as 100 gallons of water by doing so!

W is wasting water—
    far more than you think!
A rain cloud can be just as useful
        as a kitchen sink.

When washing dishes, bathing,
        or helping to clean the car,
be careful of how much you use.
        Make less water go far.

Organic gardening is a way of growing plants that conserves natural resources and limits the effects on the environment. It is basically chemical-free gardening, which is better for your body and better for the planet. Every year tens of millions of pounds of fertilizers and pesticides are used on American lawns. When our shoes bring these potentially harmful toxins into our homes, it can lead to serious health problems.

Xeriscaping is a method of creative landscaping that conserves water ("xeros" is the Greek word for "dry"). By adding compost that absorbs and retains water, by selecting plants that have low water requirements, and by simply watering efficiently, your family can cut your water usage in half. By selecting plants that are native to your area, rather than exotic ones that can be invasive to the local environment, you reduce the need for chemical fertilizers or potentially dangerous pesticides. The native plants and shrubs that you use can also offer familiar habitats for local wildlife, including birds and butterflies.

X is for xeriscaping,
a way of designing your yard
that allows less water use.
It's really not so hard.

Plant an organic garden
full of fruits and flowers.
It's the natural way to make use
of Earth's creative powers.

Y? The question is: Y not?
That letter stands for you.
Perhaps by reading all these rhymes
you'll know just what to do.

Maybe when you're older,
you'll help spread the news
to people far and wide
in whatever job you choose.

Many different professions revolve around protecting the planet. For instance, you could be an attorney who makes sure that environmental laws are applied, an environmental engineer or architect, or perhaps a journalist who researches and writes about the subject. You could also work for an earth-friendly organization like the Natural Resources Defense Council, the Rainforest Alliance, the Nature Conservancy, or the Clean Water Fund.

Of course, many jobs also allow workers to spend time enjoying the wonders of nature. Camp counselors introduce kids to those wonders. Park rangers help to protect the world's natural treasures—from the Grand Canyon in Arizona to the Great Barrier Reef in Australia. Wildlife biologists study animals and how changes may impact their populations. Conservation scientists develop plans to protect natural resources like rivers and rangeland. Toxicologists examine the impact of various chemicals that might affect people's health. Could one of these jobs be right for you someday?

Yy

In a single year, the average American is responsible for emitting about 20 tons of carbon dioxide into the atmosphere just as a result of everyday behavior. There are many websites that will measure your "carbon footprint" by finding the amount of carbon dioxide that is produced by your home energy use, diet, and transportation. One of the latest trends in earth-friendly living is the purchase of "carbon offsets" and "clean energy credits" to make up for the pollution you cause. Or you can plant trees to make up for it, too. The Conservation Fund's Go Zero™ program, for instance, will plant one tree for every $5 donation. Even the National Football League has gotten into the game. At the 2008 Super Bowl in Phoenix, Arizona, the league's fleet of 3,000 ground transportation vehicles produced approximately 350 tons of greenhouse gases. So the NFL planted thousands of trees in Arizona forests. Of course, the best solution is to simply live earth-friendly and make that carbon footprint as small as possible!

We all leave a carbon footprint
in our daily routines.
How much pollution each of us causes
is what that number means.

If you really want to be
an environmental hero,
just try to get your carbon footprint
down toward Z for zero.

Web Resources

Battery disposal:
www.batteryrecycling.com
www.ehso.com/ehshome/batteries.php

Carbon footprint calculation:
www.zerofootprintkids.com

Carbon offsets:
www.carbonfund.org
www.terrapass.com

Cleaning up a broken CFL:
www.ct.gov/dph/lib/dph/cfl_fact_sheet_final.pdf
www.lamprecycle.org

Clean waterways:
www.cleanwaterfund.org
www.cousteau.org
www.greatgarbagepatch.org
www.riverkeeper.org

Climate crisis:
www.fightglobalwarming.com
www.wecansolveit.org

Eating local, sustainable foods:
www.eatwellguide.org

Environmentally-friendly toys:
www.greentoys.com
www.plantoys.com

Making good buying decisions:
www.ibuydifferent.org

Organic farming:
www.rodaleinstitute.org

Rainforests:
www.rainforest-alliance.org
www.rain-tree.com

Reducing junk mail:
www.ciwmb.ca.gov/wpw/home/junkmail.htm
www.donotmail.org
www.newdream.org/junkmail
www.obviously.com/junkmail

Reusable bags and containers:
www.reusablebags.com

Reusable lunchboxes:
www.laptoplunches.com

Vermicomposting:
www.journeytoforever.org/compost_worm.html
www.kids.niehs.nih.gov/worms.htm

Water footprint calculator:
www.h2oconserve.org

General information:
Animal Planet: www.animal.discovery.com
The Conservation Fund:
    www.conservationfund.org
Eartheasy: www.eartheasy.com
Earth Friendly Fundraising: www.greenraising.com
Environmental Defense Fund: www.edf.org
Greenpeace: www.greenpeace.org
National Geographic's Green Guide:
    www.thegreenguide.com
National Institute of Environmental Health
Sciences Kids' Pages:
    www.kids.niehs.nih.gov/home.htm
National Wildlife Federation: www.nwf.org
Natural Resources Defense Council:
    www.nrdc.org
The Nature Conservancy: www.nature.org
Sierra Club: www.sierraclub.org
Wildlife Conservation Society: www.wcs.org
Worldwatch: www.worldwatch.org
World Wildlife Organization:
    www.worldwildlife.org

Websites just for kids:
Children of the Earth United:
    www.childrenoftheearth.org
Earth Matters: www.earthmatters4kids.org
EcoKids: www.ecokidsonline.com
Eekoworld: www.pbskids.org/eekoworld/
Environmental Education for Kids! (EEK!):
    www.dnr.state.wi.us/org/caer/ce/eek
EPA Climate Change Kid's Site:
    www.epa.gov/climatechange/kids
EPA Kid's Club: www.epa.gov/kids
EPA Student Center: www.epa.gov/students
Field Trip Earth: www.fieldtripearth.org
Flying WILD: www.flyingwild.org
The Green Squad: www.nrdc.org/greensquad
Kids' Planet: www.kidsplanet.org
Kids Saving Energy: www.eere.energy.gov/kids
National Geographic Kids:
    www.kids.nationalgeographic.com
Nature Challenge For Kids:
    www.davidsuzuki.org/kids
Planet Slayer:
    www.abc.net.au/science/planetslayer
Recycle City: www.epa.gov/recyclecity
The Story of Stuff: www.thestoryofstuff.com
Treetures: www.treetures.com
United Nations Environment Programme's
Tunza for Kids:
    www.unep.org/tunza/children
WebRangers: www.nps.gov/webrangers
Wildlife Conservation Society's Kids Go Wild!:
    www.kidsgowild.com
World Meteorological Organization:
    www.wmo.int